WORLD MYTHS AND LEGENDS

African

W9-AVH-306

Joanne Suter

Fearon/Janus
Belmont, CA

Simon & Schuster Supplementary Education Group

World Myths and Legends

Greek and Roman
Ancient Middle Eastern
Norse
African
Far Eastern
Celtic
Native American
Regional American

Series Editor: Joseph T. Curran
Cover Designer: Dianne Platner
Text Designer: Teresa A. Holden
Interior Illustrations: James Balkovek
Cover Photo: Lowie Museum of Anthropology,
    The University of California at Berkeley

Library of Congress Catalog Card Number: 91-72589

ISBN 0-8224-4639-1

Printed in the United States of America

1. 9 8 7 6 5 4 3 2

CONTENTS

An Introduction to African Myths and Legends

Africa is a huge continent and is home to many groups of people. Most of those living in the northern part of Africa have followed the Islamic and Christian religions. The myths in this book come from groups of people who lived south of the Sahara Desert. Each group had its own beliefs, but many themes were repeated from culture to culture.

Most of the ancient African cultures didn't have written languages. They were isolated from the rest of the world by vast deserts and tropical forests.

We have these stories today because the Africans were storytellers. They had an *oral*, or spoken, literature. The stories were passed down through the generations. They weren't written out and collected until modern times.

African myths give order to the world. They explain how it began and how people came to live here. They speak of the appearance of evil in the world. They explain birth and death. But the myths do more than explain. They point to the power and mystery we feel in our lives. They wake us up to these qualities.

While these myths come from different parts of Africa, most are based on belief in a supreme creator of the universe. According to many of them, God once lived on earth. But some human or animal fault forced God to leave here and go to live in heaven. Death is also blamed on a mortal mistake. Many of the myths say it didn't always exist.

Animal tales are also popular, thanks to the many different kinds of animals that roam the African continent. In these tales, the animals are described as being like humans. Some animals are good, and some are wicked. Some are wise, others foolish. A spider is too clever for his own good and must pay for his trickery. A big fish who is too proud learns to be humble. Animal tales tell about what is best and what is worst in human beings.

Yoruba, Krachi, Ibibio, Dagomba . . . these are some of the peoples whose stories fill this book. In modern times, new religions have come into every part of Africa. Many people have turned to them. Others practice older beliefs. These myths still influence the way they look at and live their lives.

Olorun, Creator of Life

Different societies have different stories of how the earth and its people were created. This creation myth is from the Yoruba of Nigeria. Yoruba myths tell of many gods. The greatest was Olorun, Owner of the Sky, Creator of Life.

In the beginning, the sky was filled with gods. Olorun was the supreme god. He was Owner of the Sky and ruler of all that was. Below the sky was a marshy wasteland. The world was water and oozing mud.

"Let's go down and look about," Olorun suggested one day.

So the gods slid down to earth on long spiders' webs. These filmy spider's webs became bridges for the spirits of the sky. The gods played in the marshy land. They were very light and did not sink into the soft ground. But no human beings could live under the sky until there was firm land for them to walk upon.

Olorun saw that the earth was a very lonely place. So he called upon Great God. "I think you should make some firm ground under the sky," Olorun told Great God.

Then Olorun gave Great God a snail shell. Inside the shell was some loose earth. The shell also held a hen with five toes and a pigeon.

Following Olorun's directions, Great God slid down a spider's-web bridge. He carried the shell with him and scattered the earth about. Then he put the five-toed hen and the pigeon on the ground. The two birds scratched and pecked and spread the earth everywhere. Then they walked about, tromping it down. Solid ground was soon formed.

Great God watched the work. Then he climbed back up the spider's web to report to Olorun. "It is done," said Great God. "The earth is formed, and it is hard and firm."

"Well done," Olorun said. But he knew that Great God's work had to be tested. So he sent a Chameleon down to inspect it. Now the Chameleon is a slow and careful creature. Olorun knew it would inspect the earth closely.

When Chameleon went down the spider's web, he was blue in color. He was blue as the sky and blue as water. As he slowly walked about on the earth, Chameleon's color began to change. Soon he was brown, as brown as the earth.

"The earth," said Chameleon when he reported to Olorun, "is wide. But," he added, "it is still not dry enough."

Olorun sent the Chameleon to earth a second time. This time he came back with a better report. "Now," he said, "the earth is both wide and dry."

Olorun gave the newly created place a name. He called it Ifé, which meant "wide." And on Ifé, he created Ilé, which meant "house." All future houses would come from this first Ilé.

It had taken four days to create the earth. On the fifth day, Great God was honored for the job he had done.

Then Olorun said, "There is still more work to be done. Great God, go back to Ifé. Prepare for the coming of humans. They will need food and drink."

Great God planted palm trees on Ifé. The palm trees would give the humans food and drink. After the trees were planted, the rains came down to water them.

Then Great God returned to the sky. Olorun said to him, "You have done well. I will trust you to make the human bodies."

So Great God set to work. He made the bodies out of earth. He carefully molded the arms, the legs, and the heads. Then he took the bodies to Ifé. The figures were finely built, but they were not alive. Olorun, the Creator, Owner of the Sky, would give the humans life.

Great God grumbled and complained to himself. "I made the figures," he mumbled. "I should be the one to bring them to life."

Great God decided to watch and see just how Olorun made the humans come to life. So he hid among the human figures, planning to spy on Olorun.

But Olorun was not to be tricked. He knew everything and could see everything. Olorun put Great God into a deep sleep. When Great God awoke, the human beings had come to life! And Great God had no idea how Olorun had done his work.

To this day, Great God only makes the bodies of men and women. It is left to Olorun, the Creator, to give them life. And sometimes Great God still feels jealous. Then he leaves marks on the bodies to show his unhappiness.

1. *What was inside the snail shell that Oloron gave to Great God?*

2. *What did Great God use to make the human bodies?*

3. *Why did Olorun put Great God to sleep?*

Nyambi, the Creator, Leaves the Earth

Some African myths say that in the beginning, God lived among humans. He talked to them and helped them. But later God decided he had to leave the earth.

This myth comes from the Lozi people of Zambia. The Lozi called God by the name of Nyambi. Their story explains how people drove Nyambi from the earth.

In the old days, Nyambi lived on earth with his wife. Nyambi was God, and he created all things. He made the birds, the fish, and all the animals.

Nyambi also made human beings. The first man's name was Kamonu. Kamonu saw Nyambi's greatness and wanted to be just like him. Kamonu copied everything Nyambi did. When Nyambi worked with iron, Kamonu worked with iron. When Nyambi worked with wood, Kamonu worked with wood. Nyambi saw this and worried that Kamonu was trying to be a god.

Then Kamonu made a spear. With it he killed a large antelope.

"You have done wrong!" Nyambi said angrily. "You've killed one of your brothers!" With this, Nyambi sent Kamonu away to another region.

But after awhile Nyambi's anger faded, and he let Kamonu return. Nyambi gave Kamonu some land. He taught him to farm. This, he thought, would keep the man calm and give him something useful to do.

All went well for a time. But one day some buffaloes broke into Kamonu's farm. He took his spear and killed them. When deer ran through the farm, he killed them, too.

Then trouble and sorrow came to Kamonu's family. His pot broke. His dog died. Finally, when his child died, Kamonu went to talk to Nyambi. He was very surprised to see that his pot, his dog, and his child were all there, unharmed, with Nyambi.

"You have powerful medicine, Great Father—strong magic. Give me some!"

But Nyambi would not give the man any of his power. Kamonu went away grumbling.

Then Nyambi spoke to his wife. "Kamonu knows where I live," Nyambi said. "He will keep coming here and bothering me. We must move away." So God and his family went to live on an island in a river. But Kamonu built a raft and poled his way to the island.

Then Nyambi moved his family to the top of a very high mountain. But Kamonu followed him there, too.

Now by this time the population on earth was really growing. The humans were having more and more children, and Nyambi said, "I can't get away from them!"

So Nyambi called to the birds. "Fly," he said. "Find me a place where I can get away." But the birds could not find such a place.

Then Nyambi called an old man who could see into the future. "Send for Spider," the old man told Nyambi.

Spider found a new place for Nyambi to live. Spider spun a slender thread that reached right up from the earth to the sky. Nyambi and his family climbed the thread and made their home on high. They have stayed there ever since.

"Put out Spider's eyes," warned the old man who could see the future. "If you do not, Spider will show Kamonu the way to heaven." So Nyambi blinded Spider.

But still Kamonu would not give up. He kept trying to reach God. He called on some other men, and together they chopped down many trees. They made a great pile of them. "It will reach to the sky!" Kamonu exclaimed. "We'll climb up it and reach God."

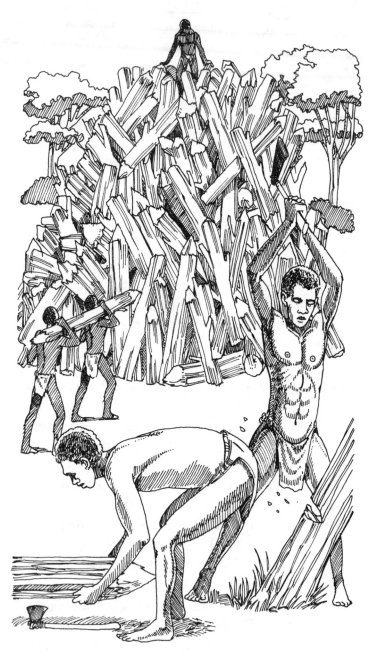

Kamonu tries to reach God

The pile of trees grew and grew until it almost touched the sky. But its size and weight became too much. Soon . . . crash! The pile fell, and trees went rolling in every direction.

And so Kamonu, the first man, never did find a way to reach Nyambi in heaven. But every morning when the sun came up, he and the other human beings would greet God. "There rises Nyambi," the people sang. "God has come!"

1. *Who was the first man that Nyambi created?*

2. *Where did Nyambi and his wife first go to escape?*

3. *Why did the old man warn Nyambi to blind the spider?*

A Higher Sky

Many African myths tell of a time when God was the low-hanging sky. Men working in the fields had to be careful not to touch God when they raised their hoes. Women pounding grain had to be careful when they raised their pounding sticks. The following story comes from the Krachi people of Togo in West Africa.

God Wulbari was the great creator. He was the sky and the heaven. He spread himself out in all directions, less than five feet above the earth's surface.

"Ouch!" cried Wulbari many times every day. For when a man would stand up, he'd often bump his head against God. People didn't seem to mind, but God Wulbari thought it very rude indeed.

Once an old woman was pounding grain for her family's bread. She raised her pounding stick, then smashed it down upon the grain. Each time she raised her long stick, she brought it up a little higher. At last, her stick poked God Wulbari right in the eye!

"Ouch!" Wulbari cried. "I had better raise myself up a bit!"

And so he did. But he was still quite close to the earth. And, it seems, people came to know God so well they took him for granted. Children wiped their hands on the sky when they finished their suppers. Once someone even tore a piece of blue right out of the sky to add to a soup. "It gives it some flavor!" the cook declared.

"I've had enough!" God Wulbari finally exclaimed. "I won't be used as a towel, and I won't be an ingredient in soup!" The angry god rose higher and higher. He stretched out beautiful and blue and out of everyone's reach. And so it has been ever since.

1. *How close was God Wulbari to the ground?*

2. *Why did the people take God for granted?*

3. *What did the cook add to the soup? Why?*

Mantis, Bee, and the First Bushman

The praying mantis was the god of the Bushmen of the Kalahari Desert. It is born a crawling worm and later changes into a winged insect with long legs. The Bushmen believed that Mantis created all things. They tell many stories about his adventures. Sometimes Mantis appears as a person and sometimes as an animal. He is always god-like in his powers.

Mantis was there at the very beginning of the world. A Bee carried him over the dark churning waters that covered the earth. Bee flew and flew and at last grew tired. His wings were cold, for there was only night and the wind. There was no warm sun.

"I cannot carry you much longer," Bee told Mantis. "I am afraid that my wings will fail and I'll drop you into the sea."

Bee looked for a safe place to set Mantis down. He flew low over the waters, searching for a bit of solid land. But there was none.

At last Bee spotted a large white flower floating on the sea. It was half open and stood out brightly against the dark water. With a

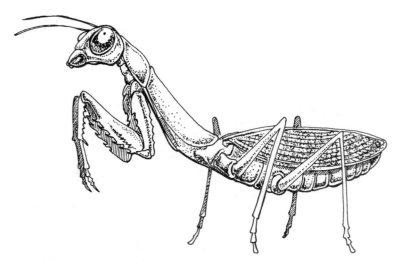

Mantis

sigh of relief, Bee laid Mantis in the heart of the flower. Bee and Mantis also planted in the flower the seed of the first human being. Weary Bee then died. But the sun of the first morning rose, and the flower opened wide. There was Mantis, alive and well in the light of day. And there, too, the first Bushman was born.

1. *What is a praying mantis?*

2. *What carried Mantis over the dark churning waters?*

3. *Where was Mantis dropped?*

The First Man

This creation myth comes from the Fang people of Gabon. It describes human beings in two parts. The body is called Gnoul. The soul, or everlasting shadow, is called Nsissim.

In the beginning there were no people. There were no animals, plants, heaven, or earth. There was only God, and he was called Nzame. Nzame was three gods in one: Nzame, Mebere, and Nkwa.

First heaven and earth were made by Nzame. Then he blew on the earth, and water was created too.

Nzame made everything. He made the sun, moon, stars, animals, and plants. When he had finished, he asked Mebere and Nkwa, "Have I left anything undone?"

Mebere and Nkwa looked about. They said, "We see many animals, but we do not see their chief. We see many plants, but we do not see their master."

So Nzame, Mebere, and Nkwa chose creatures to serve as masters. They chose the Elephant because he had wisdom. They chose the Leopard because he had power and cunning. They chose the Monkey because he was quick and nimble.

But Nzame saw that something was still missing. And so the three that were Nzame created a being that was very much like themselves. One gave the new being force. The second gave the being power to rule. The third gave the being beauty. Then the three said to the being, "Take the earth. You are now the master of all that is. Like us, you have life. All things belong to you."

Nzame, Mebere, and Nkwa called this first human Fam, which means "power."

Nzame, Mebere, and Nkwa went back to live on high, and Fam stayed below. Everything on earth obeyed him. But the Elephant remained the most powerful animal. The Leopard remained the second most powerful, and the Monkey the third.

Fam enjoyed his position as master of the earth. He had might and beauty. But in time, this first man became proud of himself. He didn't want to worship Nzame.

"God is God, man is man," sang Fam. "Everyone in his house; everyone for himself."

Nzame heard the song and became very angry. "I will teach you to turn away from God!" Nzame called for Thunder.

"Boom, boom, boom!" Thunder came running when Nzame called. And the fires of heaven fell on the forest. Fam's newly planted farm burst into flames. Animals, birds, and fishes were all destroyed.

But when Nzame created Fam, he had made him a promise. "You shall never die," God told Fam. And God never goes back on his word.

Fam was burned badly, but he lived. The fire, however, had frightened him. So he ran away and hid.

The world was now black and empty. "What have we done?" asked Nzame, Mebere, and Nkwa. "We must do better!"

So they covered the burned land with a new layer of earth. A new tree sprang up, and it was bigger and better than any before. When a leaf fell from the tree it grew and grew. It began to walk. It was an animal. When a leaf fell into the water, it swam. It was a fish. The earth became again what it had been, and what it is today.

"Now we shall make another man like Fam," said Nzame. "He shall have the same legs and arms. But this man shall know that someday he must die."

This second man was to be the father of all humans. Nzame called him Sekume.

Nzame did not want to leave Sekume alone on earth. "Make yourself a woman from a tree," Nzame told him.

Sekume made a woman, and he called her Mbongwe.

Nzame saw to it that Sekume and Mbongwe had two parts. Each had an outer part called Gnoul. This was their body. The other part lived within the body. It was called Nsissim.

"Nsissim is the shadow and the soul," Nzame explained to Mebere and Nkwa. "It is Nsissim who makes Gnoul live. Nsissim goes away when man dies. Nsissim leaves the body, but he does not die. And do you know where Nsissim lives within you? He lives in the eye. The shining point in the middle, that is Nsissim. The soul is in the eye."

Then Nzame found Fam, the first man, in his hiding place. Nzame remembered how Fam had turned away from him. So he locked him away beneath the earth. There Fam grew angrier and angrier. He also grew more evil. At last Fam tunneled his way out of his underground prison.

"What?" Fam cried when he returned to the surface. "A new man has taken my place!" Fam was furious. To this very day, he hides in the forest waiting to kill humans. He hides under the water to sink their boats. Fam is always waiting to bring trouble and misfortune.

1. *What were the names of the three gods of Nzame?*

2. *How was Fam different from the newer humans?*

3. *What were the two parts of Sekume and Mbongwe called?*

Naba Zid-Wendé

This tale comes from the Mossi people of Upper Volta. It tells of the great Naba, or Lord, who created everything. The story explains how human greed brought evil into the world. It describes how people were separated into groups. Some became masters, others slaves.

Naba Zid-Wendé and the Beginning of Time

There was no day. There was no night. There was no time. There was only the Kingdom of Everlasting Truth. It was ruled by Naba Zid-Wendé.

Naba Zid-Wendé were not one, but many, and They were very powerful. The time came when They made earth. Then They created day and night. For day, They made the sun. For night, They made the moon. And in this way, They made time.

At first, the whole earth was covered with fire. Then Naba Zid-Wendé blew Their breath over the fire. Their breath cooled the flames. Then Naba Zid-Wendé ordered Fire to live within the earth's belly.

Fire did not like living deep undergound. "I want to light the earth as the sun does!" Fire exclaimed. But Naba Zid-Wendé had already decided the way things should be. They set heavy mountains on top of the earth to hold Fire deep below.

Then Naba Zid-Wendé wanted to test the surface of the earth. They had decided to create human beings, and the earth had to be ready. So Naba Zid-Wendé made a chameleon. They sent the chameleon walking on its light feet across the earth. "Lom-lom, lom-lom," went the chameleon.

But the earth was still soft. So Naba Zid-Wendé made a cat and a lion to walk the earth. "Bonn-bonn, bonn-bonn," their heavier feet stomped down the ground. The earth became firmer.

Then Naba Zid-Wendé made snakes. The snakes crawled across the earth, which had cooled off and did not burn them. Naba Zid-Wendé also made an elephant, a rhinoceros, and a buffalo. The big animals walked heavily, "Bang! bong! bang! bong!" The earth was now strong and firm and good.

Then Naba Zid-Wendé were ready to create humans. They made the humans black. "Black is a strong color," said Naba Zid-Wendé. They blew Their breath upon the humans and gave them souls that would never die.

Naba Zid-Wendé were happy. They smiled, and Their smile became the sky. The sky hung low, within arm's reach of the human race. Every day and night people could eat a piece of the sky. This is how they nourished themselves.

1. *What was the first creature that Naba Zid-Wendé sent to test the earth?*
2. *Why did Naba Zid-Wendé make the first humans black?*
3. *What kind of souls did Naba Zid-Wendé give the humans?*

Human Greed

Naba Zid-Wendé made gold and silver stars in the sky. They made many wonderful things. At first the people were happy with the wonders around them. But in time they came to want more than they had.

"We see the earth around us. We see the sky close above. But what is below the earth?" the humans wondered. "What is under the big mountains? Perhaps Naba Zid-Wendé is keeping something from us. Perhaps the most wonderful things of all lie below."

So the people went up on top of the big mountains. There they unlocked the earth's belly. They expected something wonderful to come out. But all that crawled out was one poor, sick man. He was so full of disease that his arms and legs were wasting away.

"What is this?" the disappointed people cried. Before they could speak another word, however, the sick man lifted his arms, which turned into glowing logs. Then the logs burst into flames. Fire had disguised himself as a man.

But Fire was Evil itself, and he was jealous of the humans. The humans were allowed to eat the sky and to live under the smile of Naba Zid-Wendé. Fire was kept locked up under the earth.

In his anger, Fire reached up and burned the sky. Then the sky knew pain. The sky, the smile of Naba Zid-Wendé, rose high out of reach. Up, up, up it flew to the Kingdom of Everlasting Truth, home of Naba Zid-Wendé.

Humans had disobeyed Naba Zid-Wendé and unlocked Fire. Fire had sent the sky way up high, out of reach. Now the humans had nothing to eat.

But Naba Zid-Wendé were very forgiving. They were not angry with the humans. Naba Zid-Wendé created clouds to make rain. They made rivers and streams. And They made fruit-bearing plants and trees so that people would have food.

Naba Zid-Wendé wanted the humans to wash away the greed that had made them unlock Fire. So They made a big lake with blue water.

But the people ignored the lake. They were still greedy. Now they were trying to take everything from the plants and trees. And Evil was tossing the magic powders of hatred, wickedness, and envy into the lake.

Naba Zid-Wendé saw all this happen. The lake held evil now. It would have to be destroyed. So They commanded the sun to burn down on the water and drink it all up.

"What is happening?" the people cried. Suddenly the lake became very important to them. They ran to it before it disappeared. They wanted to bathe in it.

The first group of people dove into the lake at night. They bathed and swam. When they came out, their skins were white as the moon, from their heads to their toes.

At dawn, a second group went to the lake and dove in. They bathed and swam. When they came out, their skins were yellow!

The sun burned brighter and hotter. It drank more water from the lake. In the

The lake would disappear

middle of the day, a third group dove into the shrinking lake. They came out with skins red as copper, from heads to toes.

By evening the sun had drunk all the lake's water. Only a few puddles were left here and there. A fourth group came. They dipped their feet and hands into the puddles. They washed their mouths. When they were done, the soles of their feet, the palms of their hands, and their gums were yellow, white, or red. The rest of their skin remained black.

Naba Zid-Wendé decided They had to come according to their new colors. The people called these communities "races."

Naba Zid-Wendé saw that the humans were taking over the earth. They were carving it into pieces called countries. The stronger people called themselves masters, chiefs, and kings. They made the weaker people their slaves. They didn't remember to praise Naba Zid-Wendé, and Naba Zid-Wendé were very, very sad.

4. *Why did the people let Fire escape?*

5. *Why did Naba Zid-Wendé decide that the lake had to be destroyed?*

6. *What happened to the first group of people who bathed in the lake?*

Sun, Night, and Moon

A story from Cameroon tells of a time when many suns shone in the sky. But they did not always smile on the people of earth.

Once upon a time, there were many suns in the sky. Some were big, and some were small. Some were yellow, and some were blue. Day lasted all the time, for when one sun rested, the others were awake and shining. The earth was bright and warm, and everyone was happy. When the rain fell, it fell softly. All the people and animals thought life was good.

But one day the suns held a meeting. No one knows why they got together, but they did. They decided to shine very fiercely. The earth became hotter and hotter. The rain stopped falling. The country dried up.

Animals began to die. People began to die. They died because no food would grow. They died of thirst. Some people died because they were so frightened. They couldn't understand what was happening to their world.

At this same time, a young man was off hunting in the forest. The forest was very thick, so the suns weren't able to shine fiercely there. The hunter didn't know what was happening to his village and his family.

After a while, the hunter decided to go home. When he came out of the forest, he found dead bodies lying along the road. He also saw people who were still living but who were almost dead. Their lips were dry and wrinkled. Their skin was burned by the blazing suns.

The young man shaded his eyes with his hand and looked up to the sky. He saw the suns shining brightly above him. The young man got so angry he placed an arrow in his bow and took aim at one of the suns.

The man was a good shot. In a moment, he had killed one of the suns. Then he killed a second sun and a third. He killed and killed and killed until there was only one sun left.

This last sun was very frightened. He ran away and hid behind some big hills. The hills covered the sun completely, and everything went black. Night came to the earth for the very first time.

While it was dark, clouds filled the sky. Rain began to fall. When the sun saw the clouds, he knew he would have another hiding place. So the sun rose from behind the hills. He went up in the sky and hid behind the clouds.

The suns began to die

The earth cooled. Food began to grow. The people and the animals started to feel happy again. But the hunter was not happy. His wives were dead. His children were dead. All his friends were dead. He couldn't forgive the fierce suns. He decided he had to kill the last of them.

The sun was feeling braver now. The people on earth seemed happy enough, and he thought it was safe to come out. So every day, the sun went very high in the sky. But every night, just to be safe, he hid behind the hills.

The hunter watched and waited. One night, a large yellow moon appeared in the sky. No one had ever been able to see it before when so many suns were shining brightly.

"It must be the sun," the hunter thought. He took an arrow and carefully aimed it.

But before he could shoot, the moon cried out. "Why do you want to kill me? What have I done? I've never hurt anyone!"

The surprised hunter put down his bow and arrow. "I am sorry," he told the moon. "I made a mistake." Then the hunter told the moon that he was very much alone. He had no family. He had no friends. And so the moon bent down and took the hunter home with her.

That hunter still watches the last sun. He wants to make sure it never shines so fiercely again. And the sun still fears the hunter. Every single night, it hides behind the hills.

1. *Why did the young hunter decide to kill the suns?*

2. *Where did the last sun hide every night?*

3. *How did the moon help the lonely hunter?*

Why the Sun and Moon Live in the Sky

The Ibibio of Eastern Nigeria describe a time when the sun and moon lived on earth. But because of the sun's foolishness, he and the moon were forced to live in the sky.

Long ago the sun and moon lived on the earth. They were very good friends with the water, who lived there too.

The sun often went to visit the house where the water lived. The water always made sure the sun had a pleasant visit. But the water never visited the sun's house.

One day the sun offered the water an invitation. "Please come and visit us! Bring your whole family! My wife and I would welcome you all to our compound."

But the water did not accept the invitation. "I'm afraid I cannot come," the water said. "Your compound is too small for us. If my family and I visited, I'm afraid we would push you and your wife right out!"

The sun felt a little insulted. "Well," he answered, "my wife and I were just about to build a new compound. It will be far larger than the one we live in now. When it is finished, will you come visit us?"

"It would have to be very, very large," the water said. "My family and I take up a lot of room!"

The sun frowned. He seemed sad. Now the water didn't want to hurt the sun's feelings. So he said, "We shall come when your new compound is finished."

The sun and moon built a beautiful new compound. It was very elegant and very large. And the water kept his promise. He brought his whole family to visit the sun and the moon.

Through the front gates and into the compound the water flowed. And with the water came fish, water-snakes, swimming bugs, and seaweed.

The water flowed here and the water flowed there. It soon filled every corner and crack in the compound. "Do you still want my whole family to come in?" the water asked.

The sun's pride had made him foolish. "Yes," he answered. "Everyone is always welcome here!"

So the water continued to flow into the compound. Rivers came. Lakes came. Streams and ponds and waterfalls all came pouring in. The sun and the moon were forced to climb up onto the roof of their hut to keep dry.

But the sun felt that he couldn't go back on his word. He'd invited the water and his family, and he wouldn't take back the invitation. "Let them all come!" he cried.

In the end, the water came up to the roof. Then the sun and moon had to go up into the sky. And they have lived there ever since.

1. *Why did the water never visit the sun's house?*

2. *Who was the sun's wife?*

3. *What made the sun foolish?*

Lights in the Sky

The sun, moon, and stars, the Bushmen say, are part of the rhythm of the universe. So, too, are we and all other beings.

The Sun Man

Long, long ago, the Sun was a man. He lived among the first Bushmen on earth. He was a large man, and when he raised his arms, a great light shone from his armpits. When the Sun raised his arms, it was day. When he lowered his arms, it was night.

Years passed, and the Sun Man grew old. He slept much of the time, with his arms tucked close to his sides. Then the world was dark not only at night, but also during the day. Plants could not grow, for they needed sunlight. People were cold.

"We cannot live this way," the people said. "We must throw the Sun up into the air. Then the light will shine down from his armpits, and we can get warm again."

An old woman spoke to the children. "Go," she said. "Find the place where the Sun

Man is sleeping. Go quietly. Do not wake him. You don't want to frighten him away. Grab him and throw him up into the air."

The children looked all around for the Sun Man. It was hard to see him, for it was very dark. But at last they did find him. The children came up to the sleeping old man on quiet feet. They took a firm hold of him. He felt hot.

Working together, the children lifted the Sun Man. They threw him high into the air. "Oh, Sun," they all cried, "you must go up, up, up. You must shine in the sky and make the earth light again."

Then the children went back home and told the old woman they had done their job.

The Sun became round and was never again a man. He shone high and bright in the sky. Since that time, he has given the people light and kept them warm.

And when the sun sets, darkness comes. Then it is time for the stars and the moon.

1. *What was the Sun originally?*

2. *Where did the sunlight come from?*

3. *Who told the children to throw the Sun Man into the air?*

The Fight Between the Sun and the Moon

Mantis created all things. Among them was the Moon. Mantis threw fire up into the sky to light the night. When the full Moon shone, the Sun saw the bright light and grew angry. He was jealous of the Moon's brilliance. The Sun followed the full Moon. "I will chase you from my sky!" he cried.

But the Moon was proud too, and he stayed right where he was. When the Sun caught the Moon, he cut pieces from him with his sharp rays. Little by little, the Moon grew smaller and smaller. But before he destroyed the Moon completely, the Sun felt sorry for what he had done. So he let the Moon keep his backbone, which was a tiny sliver of light.

"Ouch!" the Moon cried, for he was badly hurt. The Moon went away to hide his pain. But he came back again. Then he grew and grew, as he wandered through the night. At last he was once more a full moon shining brightly in the darkness. And again the Sun became angry. Again he followed the Moon and cut little pieces from him.

4. *Why was the Sun angry at the Moon?*
5. *How did the Sun hurt the Moon?*
6. *What did the Sun let the Moon keep?*

The Moon and the Hare

Long ago, the Moon sent Tortoise to the earth. "Give the people this message," Moon ordered Tortoise. "Tell them: 'as I die and return again, so shall men die and return again.' "

The Tortoise started off on his journey to earth. "As I die and return again," he recited. "As I die and return again . . ." He said the words over and over because he was afraid he would forget them.

The Tortoise traveled slowly. Just halfway to earth, he was still repeating the Moon's words. "As I return . . . No, that's not it! I return then die . . . No, that's not it, either!" Tortoise had forgotten the Moon's message! "I guess I'd better return to the sky and ask Moon to repeat himself," he thought. So the Tortoise slowly made his way back.

The Moon was angry when he learned that Tortoise had forgotten his message. "I should have known better than to ask a slowpoke like you!" he cried. Tortoise hung his head in shame.

Then the Moon called upon the Hare, who was a very swift runner. "Take this message to the people on earth," Moon said. "Tell them: 'As I die and return again, so shall men die and return again.' "

"As I die and return . . ."

Hare ran off to earth. But he found some fresh green plants there and stopped a long time to eat them. When he had finished his meal, he hurried on. But then he realized that he, too, had forgotten Moon's message.

"I can't go back and tell the Moon I've forgotten," he thought. "He was so angry with the poor Tortoise. Surely if I think hard enough, I can remember the words."

So Hare continued on his way. By the time he found the people, he was sure he had the words right. He told the people on earth: "The Moon says: 'As I die, so will you, but, unlike me, you will not return again.' "

When the Moon heard of the Hare's mistake, he was furious. "I'll teach you to mix up my words!" he cried. The Moon grabbed a piece of wood, hit Hare right in the mouth, and split his lip. Ever since then, the hare has had a split lip.

7. *Why was the Moon angry at the Tortoise?*

8. *What did the Hare stop for along his way?*

9. *What happened to people because of the Hare's mistake?*

The Daughter of the Sun
and the Moon

This story from Angola is about a man who doesn't want to marry any earthly woman. He will accept no one but the daughter of the Sun and the Moon.

The first man was named Kim-ana-u-eze. He had a proud son who was a dreamer of grand dreams. One day the young man spoke to his father of marriage.

"I do not see any woman here in the village whom I wish to make my wife," said the son. "In fact, I doubt there is anyone on earth I could love."

"Then where will you find someone to marry?" asked Kim-ana-u-eze.

"I will marry the daughter of the Sun and the Moon," the young man said firmly.

The father went away shaking his head. His son's dream seemed quite impossible.

But the son of Kim-ana-u-eze was sure he could make his dream come true. So he wrote a letter to Lord Sun and Lady Moon. In the letter he told them he wanted to marry their daughter. He asked for their blessing. Then he

40

looked for a messenger to take his letter up to heaven.

He asked many animals to carry the letter. He asked Deer, but the Deer could not go into the sky. He asked Hawk. The Hawk replied that although he could fly, he could only go halfway to heaven. Further than that was too far, he said.

The son of Kim-ana-u-eze was getting discouraged. No one seemed willing or able to carry his message. Then the Frog said to him, "I can get to heaven!"

The son of Kim-ana-u-eze laughed. "If the noble Deer and soaring Hawk can't reach heaven, how can you?"

"Give me the letter," the Frog said. "I will deliver it."

The Frog sounded very sure of himself. The young man decided to give him the letter.

Now the Frog knew a secret. Every morning, girls came down from heaven on spiders' webs to draw water from a well. Next morning, the Frog hopped into the well with the young man's letter. When the water girls dipped their pitchers in the well, the Frog swam into one of them.

The water girls returned to heaven carrying the Frog. In the palace of Lord Sun and Lady Moon, Frog jumped out of the

At the earthly well

pitcher. He hopped to a table in the throne room and placed the letter on it. Then he hid himself in a corner.

Later that day, Lord Sun found the letter. He read it to Lady Moon. They were both very impressed. "I can't imagine how a man of the earth could have delivered this," said Lord Sun. "He must be very clever."

Lord Sun sat down to answer the letter. "I will consider your request," he wrote. "But first you must bring us a sack of gold coins as a marriage gift." Lord Sun left the letter lying on the table. When no one was around, the Frog snatched it up. In the morning, he carried it back to earth with him in a water girl's pitcher.

The son of Kim-ana-u-eze was very happy when he read the King's reply. He quickly gathered the gold coins into a bag. Then he asked Frog to go back to heaven with the gift.

Again Frog hid in the well. Again he went up to heaven in a water girl's pitcher. He left the sack of gold coins on the table in the throne room. Beside it, he placed another letter from the son of Kim-ana-u-eze.

When Lord Sun and Lady Moon saw the glittering coins, they were very pleased. Then Lord Sun read the letter. "Soon I will bring my wife to my home," said the letter.

Frog returned to earth and told the son of Kim-ana-u-eze that all was going well. "You need only bring your bride to earth," he said.

But the son of Kim-ana-u-eze did not want to go to heaven himself. "You must bring the daughter of the Sun and the Moon to me," he told Frog. Then his forehead wrinkled with worry. "You're very small. Are you strong enough for the job?"

"Strength isn't always the answer," Frog said. "Leave everything to me."

Then Frog went to the well and was again carried up to heaven. That night he went to the room where the daughter of the Sun and Moon slept. He hopped up on her bed and stole both of her eyes. He tied them in a handkerchief, hid himself, and waited.

"Father! Mother!" cried the daughter of the Sun and the Moon when morning came. "I cannot see!"

Lord Sun and Lady Moon were most alarmed. Lord Sun called the royal witch doctor. "Tell me what has happened to my daughter!" he demanded.

"The man who wants to marry your daughter has put a spell on her," the witch doctor said. "If she isn't sent to him, it is certain that she will die!"

Lord Sun immediately gave the orders. Next day messengers would carry his daughter down the spider's web to meet her husband.

Early in the morning, the Frog hid again in the water pitcher. He returned to earth with the water girls, and waited beside the well. Soon the royal messengers appeared, carrying with them the lovely daughter of the Sun and Moon.

Frog gave the girl back her sparkling eyes. Then he took her to the house of the son of Kim-ana-u-eze. The young man's dreams came true. The son of Kim-ana-u-eze and the daughter of the Sun and Moon were married.

Now the wife never went back to heaven. But Frog had enjoyed going up the spider's web. So he continued to make his secret trips. Indeed, it is said that during very hard rainstorms, frogs sometimes fall from the sky.

1. How did the Frog take the message to heaven?

2. What did Lord Sun request as a marriage gift?

3. What did the Frog steal from the daughter of the Sun and Moon?

Why Spiders Hide in Corners

African mythology includes many stories about animals. The animals are described as having human feelings. Some act like "good" human beings, while others are greedy, lazy, vain, or mischievous. The stories in this part of the book tell how the animals came to be as they are.

Lazy Spider

"Spider! Wake up! Don't you think it is time to plant?"

Spider's wife shook her lazy husband from his bed. It was the rainy season, the time to plant groundnuts in the field.

"Oh," Spider yawned, "don't be in such a hurry. There's plenty of time to plant." He went back to sleep.

Days passed, and Spider's wife saw her neighbors go off to their fields. Only her husband stayed at home. Every day she asked him, "When will you begin to plant?"

"The nagging woman will never give me any peace!" Spider thought to himself. "I guess I shall have to go to the field."

So Spider told his wife to measure out

a bag of groundnuts. Then he set off for his field to plant them.

The sun was high by the time he arrived at the field. Spider was hot, thirsty, and tired. He sat down near a cool stream. He took a drink of water and began nibbling on the nuts in his bag.

Then, as he usually did after eating, Spider fell sound asleep. By the time he woke, evening had come. He hadn't done a minute's worth of planting all day. Spider took some mud from the stream and smeared it over his body. Then he headed for home.

"Oh, I am so tired and so dirty," Spider moaned to his wife. "I've worked so hard in the field today."

The wife smiled, for she was happy with her hard-working husband. She prepared a hot bath for him and a fine supper.

The next day, Spider went off to the field again. While his neighbors hoed and weeded, Spider napped beside the stream. He did this day after day. Finally the time came for gathering the groundnuts that had grown in the field.

The other husbands brought home big sacks of nuts every day.

"Where is our harvest?" Spider's wife asked. "Surely our groundnuts are ready by now!"

Spider realized that something would have to be done. So one night, as his wife slept, Spider crept off to his neighbor's field. It was a fine field indeed, for his neighbor was a hard worker. Row after row of groundnuts were ready for harvest.

Quietly, Spider stole nuts from his neighbor's field. He filled a big bag with them and then hid the bag near his own field.

Next morning, Spider exclaimed to his wife, "Today's the day! Today I'll begin to harvest our field. You can expect a big bag of groundnuts tonight. You'll see what a fine crop I've grown."

That evening Spider came home with a big bag of nuts. His wife cracked one open and took a bite. A smile spread over her face, for the nuts were indeed delicious.

Night after night, Spider stole nuts from his neighbor's field. Soon his pantry was stocked with a huge supply of them.

1. *What did Spider do instead of planting his groundnuts the first day he went to the field?*

2. *How did he fool his wife that night?*

3. *What did Spider start to do when it was time to harvest the nuts?*

The Trap

Spider's neighbor saw that his crop was disappearing. "Someone is stealing my groundnuts!" he said. "I'll catch the rascal this very night!"

The clever neighbor laid a trap for the thief. He went into the bush to find some gutta-percha trees. He made long slashes in the bark and drained the sap. Then he took the rubbery brown sap and formed it carefully into the shape of a man. He placed the rubber man right in the middle of his groundnut field. "Ha, ha!" laughed Spider's neighbor. "Soon I shall have my thief!"

That night, as he had many other nights, Spider crept from his warm bed. He made his way to his neighbor's field. By the light of the moon, he spied the strange figure in the middle of the field.

"Oh!" Spider cried. "Who are you?"

The rubber man, of course, did not answer.

"What are you doing here at this hour of the night?" Spider called.

Still he got no answer.

So Spider walked up closer to the man in the field. "Why don't you *answer* me?" Spider cried out. He was getting angry, and he was also a little frightened of the strange silent man.

Spider lifted his arm and punched the man right in the face. Now the rubber man had been standing in the field all day. The sun had made him very, very sticky. So when Spider struck the man's face, he couldn't pull his hand away.

"Let me go!" Spider cried. He hit the rubber man with his other hand. That hand stuck tightly too. Spider was in quite a fix.

"Well, take this!" Spider shouted. He kicked the rubber man with his right foot. It stuck. Then he kicked with his left. His left foot stuck. With all his limbs stuck fast to the rubber man, Spider butted at him with his head. Of course, his head got stuck too.

"No, no!" Spider cried. He tugged and tugged but could not free himself. "When morning comes, everyone will find me here. They'll know I'm a thief!"

And that is exactly what happened. Early the next morning the neighbor came to his field. He called all the other neighbors to see the rascal he had caught. Then he pulled Spider away from the rubber man and shook him soundly. "Don't you ever let me catch you in my field again!" he shouted.

Poor Spider. He was so ashamed of his thievery. Spider hurried back to his house. There he hid himself in a dark corner. He saw no one, and he spoke to no one. Since that day, spiders have always hidden in corners.

4. *What did Spider's neighbor use to make his rubber man?*

5. *Why was the rubber man so sticky?*

6. *Why did Spider hide in a corner?*

Why Spiders Are Found
in Every Corner

Many West African stories tell of Anansi and his trickery. This one explains how he came to be a spider.

Anansi was once a man. He had a large farm, and every year he grew a fine crop of corn. The king, who lived nearby, owned a wonderful ram. It was more beautiful and much larger than any other ram.

"No one is allowed to touch my ram!" the king ordered. "He may roam the kingdom freely. He can do what he wants and graze where he pleases!"

Now Anansi was very proud of his corn. This year it was especially tall. But one day when Anansi went to look at his crop, he was horrified by what he found. Part of his field had been stomped upon! Some of his corn had been eaten! And, in the middle of the field, munching away happily, stood the king's huge ram.

Anansi fell into a rage. He picked up a stone and hurled it at the ram. The stone struck the ram and killed him right away.

Anansi and the King's ram

"Oh, no!" Anansi cried, remembering the king's orders. "What have I done?"

Anansi stood under a tree wondering what would become of him. Just then, a nut fell on his head. He picked it up and ate it. Another fell. Then Anansi had an idea. He lifted the dead ram onto his shoulder and climbed into the tree with it. He hung the ram on one of the tree's branches.

Then Anansi went to call on a friend, who was a large Spider.

"Look!" Anansi said to the Spider. "I have found a wonderful nut. I'll show you where you can find many more like it." Anansi showed his friend the nut and led him back to the tree in the corn field.

"Shake the tree," Anansi said, "and many more nuts will fall."

The Spider loved nuts, so he shook the tree with all his might. Plunk! Down fell the king's ram at the Spider's feet.

"Oh, no!" Anansi cried. "Look what you've done! You killed the king's ram by shaking him from his resting place."

"Dear, oh dear!" moaned the Spider. "What shall I do now?"

"I think the best thing would be to go directly to the king. Tell him what you did. Perhaps he'll be in a good mood."

Spider picked up the dead ram and went on his way. Anansi waited with a big smile on his face.

But on his way, the Spider stopped to tell his wife what had happened. He wanted to kiss her good-bye, just in case he never saw her again.

"Fool!" Spider's wife shouted when he told her his story. "Don't you know that rams don't climb trees? Anansi has played some trick on you. You should know you can't trust that man. Here is what you must do. Go on to the king's palace, but do not see him. Then go back and tell Anansi that all is well."

So Spider pretended to visit the king. When he came back he told Anansi that the king wasn't angry at all. "He thanked me for my honesty," Spider said. "He even gave me some of the ram's meat. He told me I was always welcome in his palace."

"That's not fair!" Anansi cried. "I was the one who killed the ram. I ought to have a share of his meat!"

Then Spider and his wife seized Anansi. They took him to the king and told him all that had happened. Anansi fell to the ground and begged for mercy. But the king was furious. He kicked the man so hard that he broke him into a thousand pieces.

Those pieces became a thousand small spiders. And that is why spiders are found in every corner of the house.

1. *Why did Anansi kill the king's ram?*
2. *Where did Anansi hide the dead ram?*
3. *Why did Spider tell Anansi that the king had given him some of the ram's meat?*

Why the Dog Is a Friend of Man

This Bushong tale tells how dogs left the wild and went to live with people.

Long ago, the Dog lived in the wild. He roamed the bush with his brother, the Jackal. They hunted together, and, like true brothers, shared whatever food they caught.

Then a hard, hard winter came upon the bush. Each day the Dog and the Jackal hunted, but each night they came back with nothing. Cold wind storms blew, and the brothers could find no protection.

The Dog began to complain. "I'm hungry," he moaned. "I'm cold."

"Go to sleep," the Jackal said. "Perhaps tomorrow we'll catch a fat young deer."

The Dog curled into a ball beside the Jackal but was unable to sleep. His coat wasn't as thick as the Jackal's, and he couldn't get warm. He shivered. His stomach grumbled.

"Perhaps if I keep moving, I won't freeze," he thought. The Dog got up and circled around the Jackal. As he walked, he caught sight of a red glow in the distance.

"Wake up, Brother," he said. "What is that light in the distance?"

"It's a village," the sleepy Jackal mumbled. "That red glow is Man's fire."

"Fire?" said the Dog. "I've heard of fire. It's very warm, isn't it? Couldn't we go ask Man for some of his fire?"

"Certainly not!" replied the Jackal. "Man is no friend of ours." The Jackal turned on his side and went back to sleep.

The Dog curled up in the tightest ball on the cold bare ground. Still he could not sleep. "Maybe," he thought, "there's food in the village as well as fire."

At last the thought of warmth and food got the best of him. "I can't stand it any longer," he said to the Jackal. "I'm going to Man's village to try to get some fire. Perhaps I can get food too. I'll bring some to you. If I don't return, call loudly for me. I may have lost my way."

The Jackal growled sleepily, and the Dog went off.

The red glow of the Man's fire grew larger and brighter as the Dog ran toward it. At last he came to the village. He crept in silently, on his belly, for he was more than a little afraid. Then he sniffed the smell of food cooking and grew braver. He approached a fire. There was no one around. The logs on the fire were crackling so nicely. Just then a Man came out of a nearby hut. When he saw the Dog, he grabbed his spear and waved it in the air.

"What are you doing here?" the man cried. "Have you come to steal my food? I'll teach you to break into my compound."

"Please do not hurt me," the Dog begged. "I only came to get a little warmth from your fire. I didn't mean to take anything. Please, let me lay down and warm myself. Then I'll go back into the bush and never bother you again."

The Dog looked so cold and unhappy that the Man felt sorry for him. "You may warm yourself," the Man said. "But you must promise not to harm anyone in the village. When you're warm, you must go back into the bush."

The Dog lay down beside the fire. Before long, the Man came up and laid before him a dry old bone. Then he went into his hut. The Dog sniffed the bone and bit down on it. The fire was warm, and the bone tasted very good. The Dog had never been so comfortable in his life.

"Are you warm yet?" the Man called out from his hut.

"Not quite yet," the Dog answered. He didn't want to leave the fire. He cracked the bone with his strong teeth and began licking out the delicious marrow. Then he fell fast asleep.

"You must be warm by now!" the Man said as he woke the dog from his sleep.

The Dog looked up at the Man. "Yes," he admitted. "I am warm. But I don't want to go back into the bush. It's cold there. I'm often hungry. Won't you let me stay here with you by the fire?"

"Why should I?" the Man asked. "What can you do for me?"

"I'll go with you when you hunt. I'll help you catch birds. I promise to never bother your chickens or your goats. All I ask is a place by your fire and the bones at the end of your meal."

The Dog stared at the Man with soft brown eyes. The Man couldn't say no.

"You must promise to obey me," the Man said. "You must be loyal and faithful."

Ever since that day, the Dog has lived with Man. On some nights, the Jackal calls from the bush. He howls long and low, calling to show the Dog the way back. But the Dog, happy by the fire, does not answer his brother's call.

Calling for the Dog

1. *Why couldn't the Dog handle cold as well as the Jackal?*

2. *What promise did the Man ask the Dog to make?*

3. *Why doesn't the Dog ever answer the Jackal's call?*

Why the Crab Has No Head

The crab is an unusual-looking creature that has no head. Its eyes are attached to the main part of its body. The people of Eastern Nigeria told this tale to explain the crab's strange appearance.

The Hunt

God made the earth. Then he chose the Elephant to be king of all who lived there. The earth was green and thick with trees. But there were no rivers or lakes back in those long-ago days.

"I am thirsty," the Elephant complained. So God made him a pond where he could drink. The Elephant was a good ruler, and he shared the pond with the rest of earth's creatures.

One day the Elephant announced to the Hawk and the Crab, "Today is hunting day! Would you like to come with me?"

The Hawk was a fine hunter. He flew off to get his bows and arrows. But the Crab was a slow-moving creature and was too small to hold a bow and arrow. When the

Crab heard about the hunting trip, he was worried. How could he join in on the fun?

Next morning, the Hawk and the Elephant set off with their bows and arrows. The Crab had stayed awake all night thinking about a way that he too could hunt. Now he dragged a net along the ground to a spot he had chosen carefully. He strung the net across a path leading out of the forest. Then he waited.

Soon a cry came from deep within the forest. The Elephant and the Hawk had wounded an animal. Minutes later, the wounded beast came running from the forest, straight into the Crab's waiting net. The Crab bashed the animal over the head with a log, and it died.

The Elephant and the Hawk shot many animals that day. But only some of them died immediately. The wounded animals struggled through the forest. Most of them ended up in the Crab's net.

By late afternoon, the Elephant and the Hawk were ready to end their hunt. The Elephant had killed five antelope. The Hawk had killed three. "We had a fine day!" the Elephant trumpeted.

"It was a good hunt," the Hawk agreed. "But we really should share our fortune with the Crab. He's probably killed nothing at all today."

But then the Elephant and the Hawk came out of the forest. And they found the Crab waiting proudly beside his ten dead animals. All of the animals were many times bigger than the Crab himself.

"I can't believe it," the Hawk cried. "You're a much better hunter than I would have ever thought!" The Hawk patted the Crab on the back and told him he had done well.

But the Elephant was jealous and angry. How could a lowly Crab kill more animals than he, the King of the Earth?

"Hawk, you kill that sneaky Crab!" the Elephant shouted. "He must have cheated! He must have tricked us! Off with his head at once!"

The Crab was frightened. Perhaps he'd been too clever for his own good. "Please, mighty King," the Crab begged, "don't kill me. You can have all this meat if you only let me live. I promise you, I will never come near you again."

The Elephant thought for a moment. "Go then!" he roared. "Get out of my sight!"

The Crab moved away quickly and then lay down to calm himself. When he had stopped shaking, he began to plan his revenge.

1. *What was the Crab's plan for hunting?*

2. *Why was the Elephant angry at the Crab?*

3. *What did the Crab promise the Elephant?*

The Crab's Trick

Next morning the Crab went directly to the Elephant's home. He hid behind a tree and waited. Soon the Elephant went out. Then the Crab went into the Elephant's home to speak with his wife.

"Good woman," the Crab said, "your husband is King, and he works so hard. It's going to get very cold today. Don't you think it would be nice to make him a good hot soup? One with lots of peppers is so fine when the weather turns cold."

"That's a splendid suggestion," said the Elephant's wife. She immediately set to work on the soup.

"Lots of peppers!" the Crab said. "You can't have too many on a day like this!" When the Elephant's wife turned from her cooking pot, the Crab threw in a few extra peppers.

The Elephant's wife finished cooking the soup just before the Elephant got home for supper. When the Crab saw him coming, he shuffled away.

"Look," the Elephant said to his wife. "I've brought home my friend the Hawk. We're *cold*. Did you cook us something warm?"

"Oh, yes," his wife said. She dished up two huge bowls of the soup. The Hawk and the Elephant ate heartily. Of course, when they finished the hot and spicy soup, they were very, very thirsty.

"Let's go to the pond," said the Elephant. "I need something to drink!"

Meanwhile, the clever Crab had made his way to the pond. Working as hard as he could, he'd scooped dirt into it until there was no water left. Then, anxious to see what would happen, he'd buried himself in the sandy mud at the bottom.

The thirsty Elephant and the thirsty Hawk came to the spot they knew as the pond. "What's this?" the Elephant cried. "What's become of my pond? We'll have to dig and dig until we reach water!"

So the Elephant and the Hawk began digging up the pond, and the more they dug, the thirstier they got. Suddenly the Elephant roared with rage. He'd uncovered the Crab, and he knew right away just how he had tricked him.

"I let you go once!" the Elephant shouted. "But this time you'll pay for your mischief!" The Elephant then grabbed the Crab and— *whack!*—cut off his head. Then he threw him back into the mud.

By this time, all the digging had uncovered water. It began gurgling up from the earth, and soon the pond was filled again. The thirsty Elephant and the Hawk drank their fill. As they turned to leave, the Hawk said, "Look! The water's getting higher. I think it will overflow the pond!"

"Dig an opening at one end," the Elephant ordered. "Let some of the water run out."

The Hawk did as he was told. The water began draining from the pond in a steady stream. But the stream got wider and wider and deeper and deeper. It carved a long ditch in the ground. Soon a river was flowing downhill from the pond. It was the first river on earth.

And what about the poor Crab? In truth, he wasn't dead at all. He'd been lying blind and headless at the bottom of the pond. After a while, he realized he could still move. So he wandered about and found his way to the river. He floated down the river until he bumped into a Fish.

The Crab told his story

"What's happened to you?" the Fish asked.

The Crab told the Fish his sad story. "I wish I could help you," the Fish said. "But I can't give you a head or eyes. Perhaps my friend the Prawn could help."

The Fish led the Crab to the Prawn. "I can't help you with the head," the Prawn said. "But I do have this extra pair of eyes." The Prawn fastened his extra eyes to the Crab's shoulders.

The Crab peered this way and that. "They work splendidly!" he said. Then the Crab crawled away, leaving the pond, the Elephant, and the Hawk far behind him. Since then, not a crab in the world has had a head.

4. *How did the Crab make the Elephant and the Hawk thirsty?*

5. *What did the Elephant do when he found the Crab?*

6. *Who gave the Crab new eyes?*

Why the Bat Flies at Night

Animals in African myths often play tricks on one another. This is the story of a trick that was too cruel.

Long ago, the Bat and the Bush-rat spent much of their time with each other. During the day, they were hunting partners. At night, they took turns cooking and ate dinner together.

But the Bat didn't really like the Bush-rat. In fact, he even dreamed of cruel plots to hurt him. One day he came up with a really nasty plan.

Now the Bat could cook a wonderful soup. "Your soup is so tasty!" the Bush-rat often raved. "Why is it so much better than mine?"

The next time the Bush-rat asked this, the Bat was ready to put his plan into action. "I'll show you how to make the soup tomorrow," he said.

The Bat cooked the next day's soup as he usually did. Then he set it aside and filled another pot with warm water.

When the Bush-rat appeared at the fireside, the Bat greeted him. "Come," the

Bat said with a wicked smile. "Let me show you how I make my soup."

The Bush-rat stepped closer.

"You see," the Bat said, "I always boil myself in the soup just before I serve it. My flesh is quite sweet, and it gives the soup that extra flavor."

"No!" the Bush-rat cried in surprise.

The Bat jumped into the pot of warm water and sloshed about. "See!" he cried. Then he climbed out and shook himself off. "Hand me a towel," he said to the Bush-rat.

The Bush-rat turned away to get the towel. When he did the Bat switched the pot of warm water for the pot of hot soup. Then he served the soup to the Bush-rat.

"Yum!" the Bush-rat exclaimed. "It's as delicious as ever. If I jump into my cooking pot, will the soup taste as good?" he asked.

"Of course," the Bat answered. "You are the secret ingredient!"

The next night was Bush-rat's turn to make dinner. First he built a roaring fire. Then he filled his pot with all sorts of tasty things to eat. He hung the pot over the fire and brought the soup to a rolling boil. Then he jumped into the pot. It was the Bush-rat's poor wife who found him there, boiled to death.

Of course, she was very upset, and she ran sobbing to the village chief. "My husband is dead," she cried. "It's all the fault of the wicked Bat!"

The chief was angry. He thought the Bush-rat was a very stupid creature. But the Bat's trick was much too cruel.

"Arrest the Bat!" the chief ordered. "Bring him to me for punishment!"

The chief's servants looked everywhere, but they couldn't find the Bat. He'd heard about the search party and had gone to hide in the bush.

Days passed, and the Bat grew hungry. But he dared not hunt while it was light out. He could still hear the cries of the chief's servants as they searched high and low, trying to find him.

The Bat knew he'd die if he didn't go out to hunt. So he waited for darkness. Each night he went out. And each day he returned to hide in a hollow tree deep in the bush.

And that is why bats never fly during the daytime.

The Bat hunted at night

1. What was the Bush-rat's favorite dish that the Bat would cook for him?

2. How did the Bat keep the Bush-rat from seeing him switch pots?

3. Why did the Bat go into hiding after the Bush-rat died?

Why Apes Look Like People

Have you ever looked closely at the faces of the apes in the zoo? Do you wonder about their human-like features? This Nigerian tale explains why apes look so much like people.

The New Animal

In the very earliest days, only animals walked the earth. They all knew their friends, and they all knew their enemies. The animals lived together in a fairly peaceful world.

But this would change. It began one crisp autumn day when the Deer family went to the big lake to drink.

Bang! A loud noise cracked the air. It was louder than any noise the animals had ever heard before. In an instant, the youngest Deer fell on his side at the water's edge. Blood appeared on his soft fur. His tongue hung out of his mouth.

Most of the other Deer were frightened. They ran to the safety of the woods. Only the oldest brother remained, for he was very curious. He hid behind a tree and waited for whatever would happen next.

He heard twigs cracking and bushes rustling. Then a strange creature stepped into the clearing beside the lake. It walked on two legs and had no hair except a little on top of its round head.

The new animal carried a stick in its hand. It walked over to the dead Deer and grabbed him by his hooves. Then it dragged the poor Deer away.

The Deer's brother, watching from the bushes, was indeed frightened. Never before had he seen such a creature. He ran through the forest to catch up with his family.

"You should have seen it!" he gasped to his father. "It walked on two legs! It took my brother! It . . . it . . . it . . ." The poor Deer was too frightened to go on.

The father Deer didn't know whether to believe his son or not. But during the next few weeks he told the strange story to just about everyone he met.

"No!" they all said. "Such an animal does not exist."

But then the Robin family told a similar story. Two Robins had been out flying when they heard a loud bang. One of the Robins fell from the air. A spot of blood darkened his feathers. He was dead.

"We'll find this new animal," said the Robins and the Hawks, "and bring back more news."

So the Robins and Hawks flew off. A sharp-sighted Hawk spotted the new creature. The strange animal was standing on his two legs in a clearing. The Hawk landed in a tree, folded his wings, and settled in to watch.

First the creature placed sticks of wood in a heap. Then, it created fire! This creature could do what the lightning could do. The Hawk was impressed.

The creature took a piece of meat and put it over the fire. The meat turned black, and the creature ate it. When the creature lay down on the ground and closed its eyes, the Hawk took flight again. He flew swiftly, for he was anxious to tell the other animals what he had seen.

The animals talked among themselves for several days. What should they do about this new animal who had come to live among them? They couldn't let it continue to kill. Surely, it would live among them peacefully if it knew the rules.

"Someone must talk to the new animal," the Elephant said. "Someone must teach it our ways."

"Rabbit, you're a fast-talker," the Fish said. "Why don't you go and talk to the stranger?"

The Rabbit agreed to go. The Hawk said he would join the Rabbit on the journey. So they traveled to the clearing where the creature had last been seen.

Sure enough, there it was, standing tall on its two legs. The Rabbit hopped boldly up to the new animal. But before he could utter a word, the creature grabbed him. It held the frightened Rabbit so tightly he couldn't speak.

The Hawk, waiting high in a tree, saw everything. He gave a loud scream and dove toward the creature. His sharp claws dug into its shoulders. The creature screamed and dropped the Rabbit. The Hawk picked up the Rabbit and flew back with him to the other animals.

1. *What happened when the Deer family went to the lake to drink?*

2. *What did the new creature look like?*

3. *What did the creature do that impressed the Hawk?*

The newcomer

The Animals Visit God

"What can we do? Oh, what can we do?" asked all the earth's animals.

"We could kill it!" the Rabbit suggested.

But no one was willing to go up against the creature. They knew that its stick made loud noises and spit fire.

"Well then," Rabbit said, "we must ask God about this new animal. Perhaps He can tell us how to live with it peacefully."

The Rabbit, the Deer, and the Frog decided to journey to Heaven to visit God.

"Lord," the Rabbit began when they were finally sitting before God. "There is a new animal down on earth."

"Why, you must mean Man," God said.

"Man?"

"Yes, an animal that walks on two legs. I've had the idea for some time now, and I finally got around to making him. He's an interesting creation, don't you think?"

The Rabbit, fearful of insulting God, began stuttering. "Well," he said, "that Man-animal's causing a lot of trouble. He's down there killing this and killing that. It's gotten so we're afraid to go anywhere."

"Hmmm," God said, frowning unhappily. "Go back to earth. I can see that something will have to be done about this."

The animals went home. They told the others that things would improve. But they didn't. In fact, more of the Man-animals came. They cut down the forest. When the animals moved to a new one, they cut it down as well. They put boats on the lake. They pulled fish from the rivers. And it seemed there was nothing the animals could do to stop them.

"There's only one answer," the Rabbit said. "We must become Man-animals too. That way we'll have sticks that shoot fire. We can protect ourselves!"

The Rabbit, the Deer, and the Frog went to see God again. They told Him they wanted to become Man-animals.

God thought for awhile and then agreed. "Go back to earth," he said. "Tomorrow you'll find a big pot of oil in the middle of the forest. Whoever wishes to become a Man need only wash himself in the oil."

The Rabbit, the Deer, and the Frog hurried back to earth with the good news. When the animals heard it, most were anxious to wash in the oil and become Man-animals.

"We can ride in boats," the Fish cried.

"We can cut down trees and build houses," the Squirrel said.

"We can carry big fire-sticks!" the Deer exclaimed.

God heard the animals' plans and was very sad. What had happened to this wonderful world and the peaceful animals in it? God knew the last thing the world needed was more people.

So God hurled a thunder bolt down from heaven. It hit the pot of oil and broke it into a thousand pieces. All the oil spilled out and soaked into the ground. Only a few small puddles were left.

The animals came to look at the oily mess. They stood there in surprised silence. Only the Ape seemed able to move. He bent over a puddle and washed his face, hands, and feet in the oil. That is why, to this very day, apes look like people.

4. *Why did the Rabbit begin stuttering?*

5. *What did the animals think was the answer to their problems?*

6. *Why did God hurl a thunderbolt to break the pot of oil?*

The Fable of the Discontented Fish

A fable is a legend that points out a truth. The characters in fables are often animals who speak and act like human beings. This fable teaches a lesson about pride.

Once there was a little pond of still blue water. Smooth stones covered its bottom. A few palm trees grew on the bank of the pond and kept it shady and cool. It was a very nice spot.

In the pond lived a colony of brightly colored fish. The fish were quite small, and they lived happily in their small pond. But there was one fish who was much larger than the others. He was longer, wider, and stronger.

When the big fish looked around at the smaller fish, he thought himself mighty. He'd push through the water waving his fins and scattering the small fish in every direction. "Out of my way," he'd shout. "A fellow like me needs some room!"

The little fish didn't like the big fish very much. "He really thinks he's something!" they'd say.

One day, one of the little fish had had enough. "Hey!" he said to the big guy. "Since you're so grand, why don't you leave this little pond? Surely someone so important as yourself would be happier in the big river. There you could mix with those who are worthy of your company."

The big fish thought for a moment. It sounded like a good idea. Why should he settle for this little pond and its tiny inhabitants? He had no doubt that he was meant for finer things.

So the big fish waited until the rains came. Then the pond overflowed its banks, and its waters met the big river. In a swirl of dark flood-water, the big fish passed from the little pond into the river.

Right away, he could see that things were different there. The rocks on the river bottom were very large. The river weeds were tall. "Oh, this is fine!" the big fish exclaimed.

Just then two fish swam past him. They were *very* large—twice his own size, in fact.

"Out of the way!" the river fish shouted. "Move, little fish!"

Then three more huge fish swam toward him. "Move on! Move on!" they exclaimed.

"This is our hunting ground." They glared fiercely as they swam past.

The pond-fish was frightened. He swam behind a nearby clump of weeds and hid. From time to time he tried to swim out into the river. But whenever he did, a bigger fish forced him back into hiding.

"What have I done?" he wondered. "Why did I come to this terrible place? I must get back to my little pond."

The fish struggled against the current to reach the place where the flood-waters came from the pond. There he was beaten against the rocks again and again. But at last he got back into the pond.

He lay on the bottom, too tired to move or even speak. All the tiny fish swam by and stared. Finally, he gasped, "If I'd known what the river was like, I wouldn't have left our pond."

From that day on, the big fish never said an unkind word to the tiny fish. He never said he was too big or too grand to live with them. He never complained about his pond-world. Indeed, he was grateful to be there.

1. *Why didn't any of the small fish like the one big fish?*
2. *How did the big fish get out of the pond?*
3. *How was the big fish different when he got back to the pond?*

Tortoises, Men, and Stones

We often think death a mystery. Why do people die? What happens when they do? This Nigerian story tells how death came into the world.

God created tortoises, men, and stones. Of each, he created a male and a female. He breathed life into the tortoises and the men but not into the stones.

"You'll grow old," God told them. "But when you are very old, you will suddenly become young again." God said nothing of dying.

One day the Tortoise went to visit Heaven. "I would like to have children," he said to God.

"I have given you life," God replied. "But I said nothing about children."

The Tortoise would not give up his idea. Over and over he visited God. "I would like to have children," he repeated.

At last God saw that he would have to give the Tortoise a better answer. "Do you not know," God said, "that when the living have children, they must die?"

The Tortoise looked surprised. But still he said, "I would like to have children. Let me see my children. Then I will die."

So God gave the Tortoise his wish.

When Man saw that the Tortoise had children, he too wanted them.

God warned Man, just as he had warned the Tortoise. "When the living have children, they must die."

"Let me see my children," Man said, "and then I will die."

That is how children and death came into the world. Only the stones did not want to have children, and so they never die.

1. *What does God first say will happen to tortoises, men, and stones when they are very old?*

2. *What did the Tortoise ask God to give him?*

3. *What two things make stones different from tortoises and people?*

The Stolen Bag

There are stories from all over Africa that tell how death first appeared on earth. In this one from Sierra Leone, death is the result of a mistake a dog made.

Long, long ago there were only three people on earth. There was a man, a woman, and their baby boy.

"You shall not die," God promised the people. "When you get old, you shall have new skins for your bodies."

God put these new skins in a big bag. He called the Dog to heaven. "Take these skins to the humans," God ordered the Dog.

The Dog went off with the bundle. He was a good fellow, and he fully intended to deliver the package. But on the way he met a party of other animals. They were celebrating the harvest by feasting on rice and pumpkins.

"Join us!" the animals called to the Dog.

At first the Dog shook his head. But the other animals called to him again. "Join us for just a moment," they said.

"What could it hurt?" the Dog asked

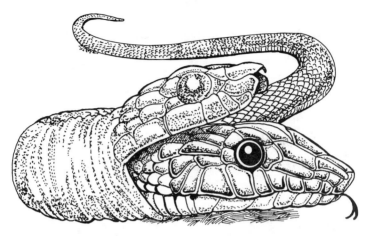

Shedding the old skin

himself. He was very hungry. The Dog put down his bundle and joined the party.

"What's in the bag?" the curious Rabbit asked.

The Dog talked about the skins he was taking to the first people. When the Snake heard the Dog's story, he slipped quietly away from the party. Then he stole the bag and carried it off to the other Snakes in his family.

"Oh, no!" the Dog cried when he got ready to leave. He looked high and low for the bag of new skins. But it was gone.

The Snakes kept the skins. Since then, humans have died while snakes have shed their old skins and gone on living. Man punishes the Snake, however, by driving

it off. Whenever he sees a Snake, Man tries
to kill it.

1. *Who did God ask to take the bag of
    skins to the humans?*
2. *Who stole the bag of skins?*
3. *What did the loss of the skins mean
    for the humans?*

Maina and the Chameleon

In this story from Kenya, death appears after a man refuses to share what he has with another.

A young man named Maina was sitting outside eating dinner. Just as the sun set, the Chameleon walked by.

"I am very hungry," the Chameleon said. "Perhaps you could give me some food."

Maina should have been a good host. He should have invited the Chameleon to share his meal. But he refused.

"Just a small bite?" the Chameleon asked. "Just a crumb?"

Maina shook his head and waved a stick to chase the Chameleon away.

"You'll be sorry," the Chameleon shouted as he left. "Because you refused me, you and all your people shall die!"

Maina was not frightened, for he didn't know what it meant to die.

The next creature the Chameleon met was a Snake. The Chameleon was still very hungry, and so he asked the Snake for food. The Snake, unlike Maina, shared his food with the Chameleon.

"Bless you!" the grateful Chameleon said. "You and your people shall live forever."

Very soon, the humans began to breathe bad air. They began to fall sick and die. The Snake, on the other hand, sheds its skin and goes on living.

1. *Why wasn't Maina frightened by the Chameleon's warning?*

2. *Who shared food with the Chameleon after Maina refused?*

3. *What was the reward for sharing with the Chameleon?*

The Many-Colored Antelope

African tales tell of ghosts, or spirits, who lived deep in the bush. Some were the ghosts of people, others of animals. Even trees had spirits.

Long ago a proud and mighty chief wanted his people to know he was greater than anyone else. So he called his hunters together one day and made an announcement.

"I will no longer ride a horse," the chief declared. "From now on, I will ride an antelope." Then the chief thought for a moment. "I won't ride just any antelope," he added. "I will ride an antelope of many colors."

"Go into the forest," he ordered his hunters. "Bring me such an animal."

The hunters searched for weeks. They found brown antelopes and black antelopes. But they couldn't find a many-colored antelope.

Then one gray morning they spotted the creature behind a tree. This was a huge antelope. His hide was dappled in soft shades of gold, brown, and white. Fog swirled all about him as he tossed his head proudly.

The hunters had little trouble catching the dappled antelope. After getting a rope around his neck, they led him to their village. What the hunters did not know was that this antelope was really a ghost.

The chief was pleased when his hunters returned. He ordered the many-colored antelope made ready to ride.

But the beast would not easily accept this. He bucked and leaped. Finally, and with much difficulty, the hunters got him saddled. The chief mounted him. At once the antelope took off. He dashed into the forest with the chief clinging tightly to his neck and back.

The hunters chased them as fast and as far as they could. But it was no use. The antelope and the chief had disappeared.

Since then, whenever that village's chief is about to die, a dappled antelope appears. He comes in the night, stands outside the chief's house, and waits to carry him away.

1. *Why did the chief want to ride an antelope instead of a horse?*

2. *What was unusual about the many-colored antelope?*

3. *What happened when the chief tried to ride the antelope?*

Pronunciation Guide

Every effort has been made to present native pronunciations of the unusual names in this book. Sometimes experts differed in their opinions, however, or no pronunciation could be found. Also, certain foreign-language sounds were felt to be unpronounceable by today's readers. In these cases, editorial license was exercised in selecting pronunciations.

Key

Capital letters are used to represent stressed syllables. For example, the word *ugly* would be written here as "UHG lee."

The letter or letters used to show pronunciation have the following sounds:

a as in *map* and *glad*
ah as in *pot* and *cart*
aw as in *fall* and *lost*
ch as in *chair* and *child*
e as in *let* and *care*
ee as in *feet* and *please*
ey as in *play* and *face*
g as in *gold* and *girl*

hy as in *huge* and *humor*
i as in *my* and *high*
ih as in *sit* and *clear*
j as in *jelly* and *gentle*
k as in *skill* and *can*
ky as in *cute*
l as in *long* and *pull*
my as in *mule*
ng as in *sing* and *long*
o as in *slow* and *go*
oo as in *cool* and *move*
ow as in *cow* and *round*
s as in *soon* and *cent*
sh as in *shoe* and *sugar*
th as in *thin* and *myth*
u as in *put* and *look*
uh as in *run* and *up*
y as in *you* and *yesterday*
z as in *zoo* and *pairs*

Guide

Anansi: uh NAN see
Bushong: BOO shahng
Cameroon: kam uh ROON
Congo: KAHNG go
Dagomba: dah GOM buh
Fam: FAHM
Fulani: foo LAH nee
Gabon: gah BON

Gnoul: guh NOOL
Hausa: HOW suh
Ibibio: ee BEE bee o
Ifé: ee FEY
Ikom: ee KOM
Ilé: ee LEY
Kalahari: kah luh HAH ree
Kamonu: kah MO noo
Kenya: KEEN yuh
Kim-ana-u-eze: keem AH nah oo EY ze
Kono: KO no
Krachi: KRAH chee
Lozi: LO zee
Luyia: LOO yah
Maina: mah EEN ah
Mbongwe: muh BONG gwe
Mbundu: muh BOON doo
Mebere: me BER e
Mossi: MO see
Naba Zid-Wendé: NAH bah ZIHD wen DEY
Nigeria: ni JIH ree uh
Nkwa: uhn KWAH
Nsissim: uhn SIHS ihm
Nupe: NOO pe
Nyambi: nee YAHM bee
Nzame: uhn ZAHM e
Olcrun: O lo ruhn

Sekume: se KOOM e
Senegal: SE nuh gahl
Sierra Leone: see ER uh ley O ne
Togo: TO go
Wulbari: wul BAHR ee
Yoruba: YOR uh buh
Zambia: ZAM bee uh